Our Furry Friends

Paintings by
JIM DALY

HARVEST HOUSE PUBLISHERS

EUGENE, OREGON

D1314025

OUR FURRY FRIENDS
Text Copyright © 2001 by Harvest House Publishers
Eugene, Oregon 97402

ISBN-13: 978-0-7369-1913-5
ISBN-10: 0-7369-1913-9

Artwork © by Jim Daly and may not be reproduced without permission.

Design and production by Koechel Peterson & Associates, Minneapolis, Minnesota

Harvest House Publishers has made every effort to trace the ownership of all poems and quotes.
In the event of a question arising from the use of a poem or a quote, we regret any error made
and will be pleased to make the necessary correction in future editions of this book.

Printed in China

07 08 09 10 11 12 13 14 15 / IM / 10 9 8 7 6 5 4 3 2 1

All things bright and beautiful,
All creatures great and small,
All things wise and wonderful,
The Lord God made them all.

Cecil Francis Alexander

He is your friend,

your partner, your defender, your dog. You are his

life, his love, his leader. He will be yours, faithful

and true, to the last beat of his heart. You owe it to

him to be worthy of such devotion.

Author Unknown

A DOG IS THE ONLY THING ON EARTH THAT
LOVES YOU MORE THAN HE LOVES HIMSELF.

Billings

Take a cat,

nourish it well with milk

And tender meat, make it a couch of silk,

But let it see a mouse along the wall,

And it abandons milk and meat and all,

And every other dainty in the house,

Such is its appetite to eat a mouse.

Geoffrey Chaucer, THE CANTERBURY TALES

A KITTEN IS IN THE ANIMAL
WORLD WHAT A ROSEBUD
IS IN THE GARDEN.

Robert Southey

My home is a haven

for one who enjoys
The clamour of children and ear-splitting noise
From a number of dogs who are always about,
And who want to come in and, once in, to go out.
Whenever I settle to read by the fire,
Some dog will develop an urge to retire,
And I'm constantly opening and shutting the door
For a dog to depart or, as mentioned before,
For a dog to arrive, who, politely admitted,
Will make a bee-line for the chair I've just quitted.
Our friends may be dumb, but my house is a riot,
Where I cannot sit still and can never be quiet.

Ralph Wotherspoon

A DOG WAGS ITS TAIL WITH ITS HEART.

Martin Buxbaum

How many

Time spent with cats is
never wasted.

Colette

times have I

rested tired eyes on her graceful little body, curled up in a ball

and wrapped round with her tail like a parcel...if they are content,

their contentment is absolute; and our jaded and wearied spirits

find a natural relief in the sight of creatures whose little cups of

happiness can so easily be filled to the brim.

Agnes Repplier

Like a graceful vase, a cat, even when
motionless, seems to flow.
George F. Will

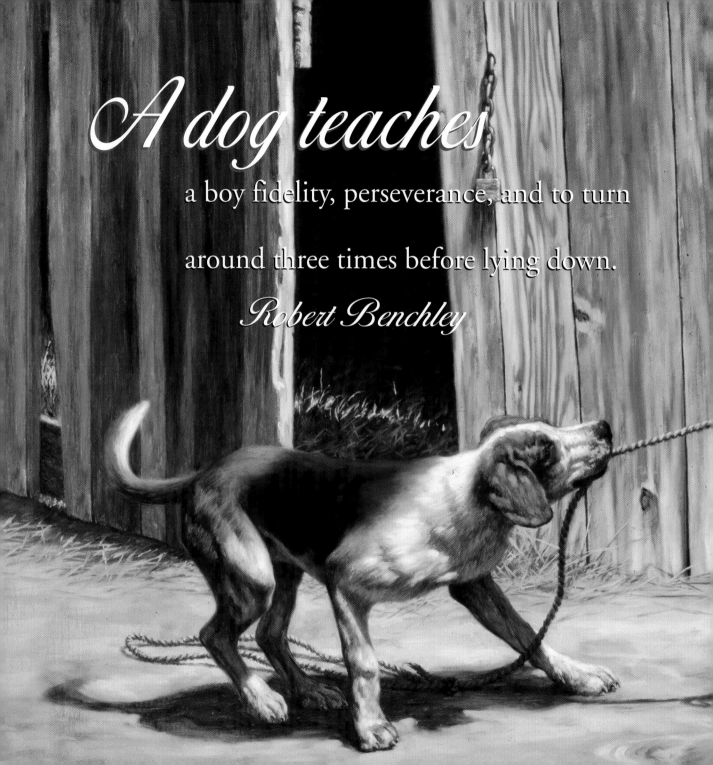

A dog teaches

a boy fidelity, perseverance, and to turn

around three times before lying down.

Robert Benchley

EVERY DOG MUST

HAVE HIS DAY.

Jonathan Swift

This most noble beast

is the most beautiful, the swiftest and of the highest

courage of domesticated animals. His long mane and

tail adorn and beautify him. He is of a fiery temperament,

but good tempered, obedient, docile and well-mannered.

Pedro Garcia Conde

THE SUNSHINE'S GOLDEN GLEAM IS THROWN,

ON SORREL, CHESTNUT, BAY AND ROAN.

Oliver Wendell Holmes

THERE IS ONLY ONE SMARTEST DOG IN THE
WORLD, AND EVERY BOY HAS IT.

Anonymous

There's just something about dogs that makes you feel good. You come home, they're thrilled to see you. They're good for the ego.

Janet Schnellman

If there is one spot of sun
a cat will find it

THERE IS NOTHING IN THE ANIMAL WORLD,
TO MY MIND, MORE DELIGHTFUL THAN
GROWN CATS AT PLAY. THEY ARE SO SWIFT AND
LIGHT AND GRACEFUL, SO SUBTLE AND
DESIGNING, AND YET SO RICHLY COMIC.

Monica Edwards

Some pussies' coats are yellow; some amber streaked with dark;

No member of the feline race but has a special mark.

This one has feet with hoarfrost tipped; that one has tail that curls;

Another's inky hide is striped; another's decked with pearls.

Carl Van Vechten

spilling onto the floor,
and soak it up.

JOAN ASPER MCINTOSH

I HAVE STUDIED MANY PHILOSOPHERS
AND MANY CATS. THE WISDOM OF CATS
IS INFINITELY SUPERIOR.

Hippolyte Taine

All of the younger children

are at present absorbed in various pets, perhaps the foremost of which is a puppy of the most orthodox puppy type. Then there is Jack, the terrier, and Sailor Boy, the Chesapeake Bay dog; and Eli, the most gorgeous macaw, with a bill that I think could bite through boiler plate, who crawls all over Ted, and whom I view with dark suspicion; and Jonathan, the piebald rat, of most friendly and affectionate nature, who also crawls all over everybody; and the flying squirrel, and two kangaroo rats; not to speak of Archie's pony, Algonquin, who is the most absolute pet of them all.

Theodore Roosevelt

Letter written to author Joel Chandler Harris in 1902

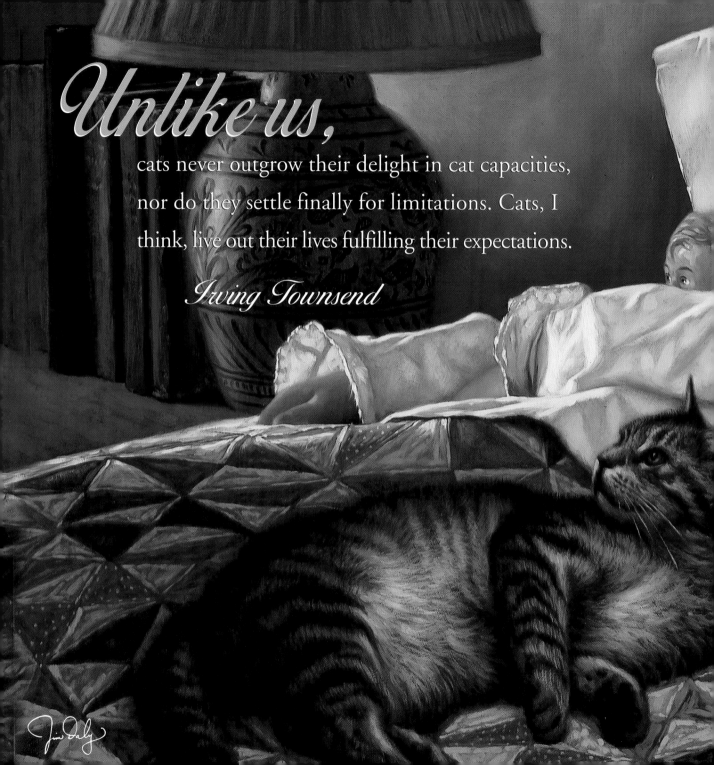

Unlike us,

cats never outgrow their delight in cat capacities, nor do they settle finally for limitations. Cats, I think, live out their lives fulfilling their expectations.

Irving Townsend

CATS ARE DESIGNATED FRIENDS.

Norman Corwin

A dog hath true love,

A dog hath right good understanding,

A wise dog knoweth all things,

A dog hath force and kindliness,

A dog hath mettle and is comely,

A dog is in all things seemly.

A knowing dog thinketh no evil,

A dog hath a memory that forgeteth not,

I say unto you again a dog forsaketh not his duty,

Hath might and cunning therewith and a great brave heart.

Gace de la Vigne

A poet's cat,

sedate and grave,
As poet well could wish to have,
Was much addicted to inquire
For nooks, to which she might retire,
And where, secure as mouse in chink,
She might repose, or sit and think.
I know not where she caught the trick—
Nature perhaps herself had cast her
In such a mould philosophique,
Or else she learn'd it of her master.

William Cowper

NEVER QUITE
FULFILLED IS
THE HOUSEHOLD
WITHOUT A CAT
OR TWO

Roger E.M. Whitaker

Dogs are not our whole life, but they make our lives whole.

Roger Caras

The reason a dog has so wags his tail

THE GREATEST PLEASURE OF A DOG IS THAT YOU MAY
MAKE A FOOL OF YOURSELF WITH HIM AND NOT ONLY
WILL HE NOT SCOLD YOU, BUT HE WILL MAKE A FOOL
OF HIMSELF TOO.

Samuel Butler

There is no psychiatrist in the world like a puppy licking your face.

Ben Williams

many friends is that he instead of his tongue.

Anonymous

No one appreciates the very special genius of your conversation as much as the dog does.

Christopher Morley

The Cats Have Come To Tea

What did she see—oh, what did she see,
As she stood leaning against the tree?
Why, all the cats had come to tea.

What a fine turn-out from round about!
All the houses had let them out,
And here they were with scamper and shout.

"Mew, mew, mew!" was all they could say,
And, "We hope we find you well to-day."

Oh, what would she do—oh, what should she do?
What a lot of milk they would get through;
For here they were with, "Mew, mew, mew!"

She did not know—oh, she did not know,
If bread and butter they'd like or no;
They might want little mice, oh! oh! oh!

Dear me—oh, dear me,
All the cats had come to tea.

Kate Greenaway

For it is by muteness

that a dog becomes for one so utterly beyond value; with him one is

at peace where words play no torturing tricks. When he just sits loving

and knows that he is being loved, those are the moments that I think

are precious to a dog; when, with his adoring soul coming through his

eyes, he feels that you are really thinking of him.

John Galsworthy

OLD DOGS, LIKE OLD SHOES, ARE COMFORTABLE. THEY MIGHT BE A BIT OUT OF SHAPE AND A LITTLE WORN AROUND THE EDGES, BUT THEY FIT WELL.

Bonnie Wilcox

You are

I THINK I COULD TURN AND LIVE
WITH ANIMALS, THEY ARE SO
PLACID AND SELF-CONTAINED.

Walt Whitman

to know then,

that as it is likeness that begets affection, so my favourite dog is a little one, a lean one, and none of the finest shaped. He is not much spaniel in his fawning, but has (what might be worth any man's while to imitate him in) a dumb, surly sort of kindness that rather shows itself when he thinks me ill-used by others, than when we walk quietly or peaceably by ourselves. If it be the chief point of friendship to comply with a friend's motions and inclinations, he possesses this in an eminent degree: he lies down when I sit, and walks when I walk, which is more than many good friends can pretend to.

Alexander Pope

Pussy Cat, Pussy Cat,

Where have you been?
I've been to London
To visit the Queen.
Pussy Cat, Pussy Cat
What did you there?
I frightened a little mouse
Under a chair.

English Nursery Rhyme

I LOVE CATS
BECAUSE I ENJOY
MY HOME; AND
LITTLE BY LITTLE,
THEY BECOME ITS
VISIBLE SOUL.

Jean Cocteau

THE SMALLEST FELINE IS
A MASTERPIECE.

Leonardo da Vinci

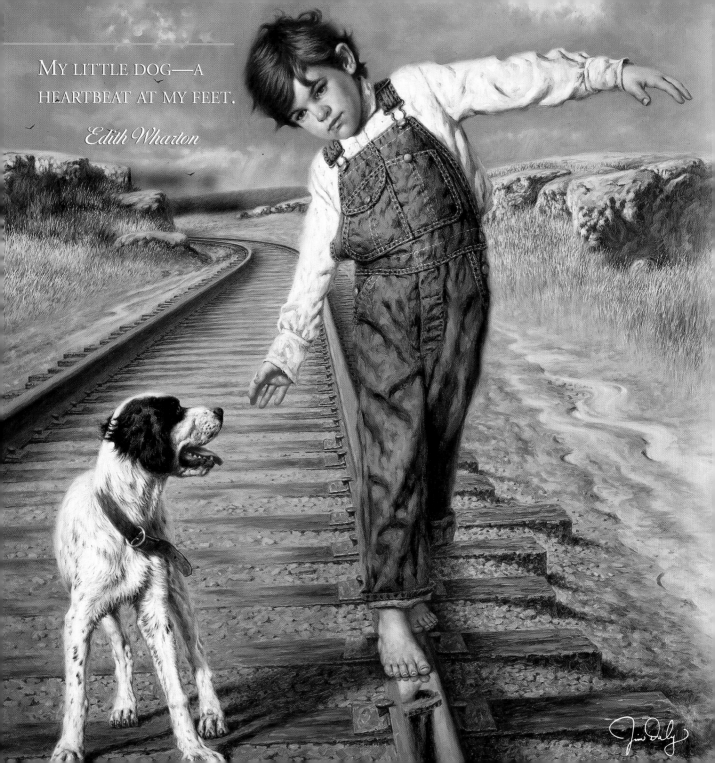

MY LITTLE DOG—A
HEARTBEAT AT MY FEET.

Edith Wharton

Yet White Fang

was never effusively affectionate. He yielded to the master's children with an ill but honest grace, and endured their fooling as one would endure a painful operation. When he could no longer endure, he would get up and stalk determinedly away from them. But after a time, he grew even to like the children. Still he was not demonstrative. He would not go up to them. On the other hand, instead of walking away at sight of them, he waited for them to come to him. And still later, it was noticed that a pleased light came into his eyes when he saw them approaching, and that he looked after them with an appearance of curious regret when they left him for other amusements...

White Fang allowed all the members of the family to pet him and make much of him; but he never gave to them what he gave to the master. No caress of theirs could put the love-croon into his throat, and, try as they would, they could never persuade him into snuggling against them. This expression of abandon and surrender, of absolute trust, he reserved for the master alone. In fact, he never regarded the members of the family in any other light than possessions of the love-master.

Jack London
WHITE FANG

He spoiled her.

Soon she would not step to the stream to drink but he must hold a bucket for her. And she would drink, then lift her dripping muzzle, rest it on his shoulder, her golden eyes dreaming off into the distance, then daintily dip her mouth and drink again. When she turned her head to the south and pricked her ears and stood tense and listening, Ken knew she heard the other colts galloping on the upland. "You'll go back there some day, Flicka," he whispered.

Mary O'Hara
MY FRIEND FLICKA

An animal's eyes have a great

Hurt no living thing:
    Ladybird nor butterfly,
Nor moth with dusty wing,
    Nor cricket chirping cheerily,
Nor grasshopper so light of leap,
    Nor dancing gnat, nor beetle fat,
Nor harmless worms that creep.

Christina Georgina Rossetti

A SMALL PET IS OFTEN AN EXCELLENT COMPANION FOR
THE SICK, FOR LONG CHRONIC CASES ESPECIALLY.

Florence Nightingale

*the power to speak
language.* MARTIN BUBER

A GOOD MAN WILL TAKE CARE
OF HIS HORSES AND DOGS, NOT
ONLY WHILE THEY ARE YOUNG,
BUT ALSO WHEN THEY ARE OLD
AND PAST SERVICE.

Plutarch

The Woodman's Dog

Shaggy and lean, and shrewd, with pointed ears

And tail cropped short, half lurcher and half cur—

His dog attends him. Close behind his heel

Now creeps he slow; and now with many a frisk

Wide-scampering, snatches up the drifted snow

With ivory teeth, or ploughs it with his snout;

Then shakes his powdered coat, and barks for joy.

William Cowper

HAPPINESS IS A WARM PUPPY.

Charles Schulz

Hear our prayer, Lord, for all animals,

May they be well-fed and well-trained and happy;

Protect them from hunger and fear and suffering;

And, we pray, protect especially, dear Lord,

The little cat who is the companion of our home,

Keep her safe as she goes abroad,

And bring her back to comfort us.

Anonymous